1. Introduction: Planning for effective learning in RE – Differentiation and assessment

The strategies for differentiation and assessment in RE are the same as any other subject but RE adds an extra dimension because the subject has an affective (feeling) element in addition to knowledge. This poses problems but also opens up possibilities.

Because RE is restricted in the amount of time accorded to it in the timetable, implementing *some types* of differentiation and assessment can be difficult. It cannot be emphasised enough that teachers can only work within what is possible for them in their context. Select from the suggestions in this book those ideas that you think will work in the time you have available.

By varying input, tasks, outcomes and assessment activities, different pupils are able to shine and their self-esteem is advanced. The pupil who may have difficulty expressing their ideas in writing can express them

through drama or art. Differentiation by task is made easier in RE because the varied nature of the subject means that different methods can be used. RE includes poetry, story telling, music, dance, drama, art, texts, buildings and food.

Note. Help with differentiation and assessment is available to teachers in the scales and guidelines provided by national bodies such as QCA and ACCAC (see resource page for more information). Some SACREs also provide guidance.

3

2.1 Differentiation: shortcuts

Differentiation is essentially a matching exercise: matching the task, resources, support and teaching style to the pupil. It is about maximising potential and meeting needs. However, RE time is short for secondary teachers who have many classes for short periods, and for primary teachers for whom RE is one subject among many. The following suggestions may help:

- Plan together with another member of staff if they are covering the same material
- Store in order to use again

- Become familiar with your resources so that you use what you have
- Organise resources – create a resource trolley/area, etc.
- Reorganise your teaching time *if possible* (longer blocks rather than short lessons)
- Use templates for lesson plans with things such as skills, attitudes, etc., already on them so that you tick boxes rather than have to write things out.

2.2 Using RE Criteria to differentiate

Both differentiation and assessment depend on having a description of the progression in knowledge, skills and understanding expected to be made or a framework to check against. The four UK nations have each provided ways of doing this.

England

QCA, in their *Non-Statutory Guidance for RE* (see resources page for details), have produced an eight level scale that largely covers skills. The content is only described in very general terms: 'stories, beliefs, practices'. This means the scale can be applied to any material. They have also produced exemplar material so that teachers have concrete examples to use but these should not be used rigidly (see http://www.ncaction.org.uk/).

Key Stage levels
- Key Stage 1 levels 1-3: by the end of KS1 most pupils with achieve level 2
- Key Stage 2 levels 2-5: by the end of KS2 most pupils with achieve level 4

- Key Stage 3 levels 3-7: by the end of KS3 most pupils with achieve level 5/6
- Level 8 and beyond is for very able pupils

Wales

The Review of Religious Education Syllabuses produced by ACCAC contains the Welsh eight level scale. See the ACCAC and Estyn websites (see resources page). The Key Stage levels are the same as England.

Scotland

Religious and Moral Education 5-14 divides the areas of study into five levels indicated by the letters a-e. Details of targets and levels can be found on http://www.strath.ac.uk/ (navigate to 'Religious and Moral Education' then select 'Resources').

- Level A should be attainable by most pupils during the years P1-3
- Level B should be attainable by some pupils in P3 or earlier but by most in P4
- Level C should be attainable by most pupils during the years P4-P6
- Level D should be attainable by some pupils in P5-P6 or even earlier but certainly by most on P7
- Level E should be attainable by some pupils in P7/S1 but certainly by most in S2

Northern Ireland

The Core Syllabus for RE has statements of attainment for each key stage. Teachers working in Northern Ireland are referred to the document *Evaluating Religious Education* published by the Education and Training Inspectorate (http://www.ucet.ac.uk/inspectorates.html).

Using levels

On an eight-level scale, the skills move from the more descriptive to the evaluative, from simple to complex, towards the increased use of higher-order skills. One of the skills that appears to be missing is creativity/expression. This can be assumed in terms such as 'recount', 'describe', and 'respond'. The outworking of these terms

can take the form of poetry, art, creative writing or drama. The response can be similarly expressive.

When planning, locate the skills (recount, analyse, etc.) with a highlighter then locate the content (stories, beliefs, etc.). When planning a piece of work, remember that you don't have to try to get in everything! You can choose just one skill and one piece of content.

AREIAC (the Association of RE Inspectors, Advisors and Consultants) has produced the levels in 'child-friendly' terms ("I can . . .") to make them easy to use, but these have not yet been approved. The statements on the scale can also be changed into "I can" statements by teachers. For example, "I can compare my ideas about life with those of believers." This might make activities easier to design.

As with any scale, including the Scottish levels, it has to be used flexibly. Some young pupils can attain high levels, while some older pupils will attain lower ones. The scale adjusts to the pupil, not the pupil to the scale. The teacher chooses higher or lower level work to fit the pupil.

2.3 Differentiation and intelligence

Howard Gardner has put forward the idea that there may be different types of 'intelligence'. He is not the only person to have done this. Some people might be more comfortable thinking in terms of talents or groupings of abilities and skills rather than 'intelligences' though that is the term Gardner uses.

If pupils differ in abilities and skills it makes sense to differentiate tasks so that different pupils can demonstrate their understanding. This does not mean trying to cater for all types of intelligence every time you teach. It means achieving a balance over a period of time. Howard Gardner lists seven or eight 'intelligences'. Seven are listed here – though there may be others:

1. **Linguistic** – good with language: its sounds, patterns and meanings

2. **Musical** – an understanding and awareness of musical patterns and rhythm

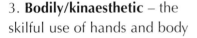

3. **Bodily/kinaesthetic** – the skilful use of hands and body

4. **Visual/spatial** – the ability to create images and to visualise, imagine or move things in space

5. **Intra-personal** – knowing oneself and reflecting on one's own feelings and behaviour

6. **Inter-personal** – good at relating to others and empathising with them

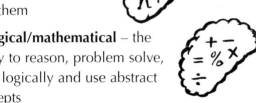

7. **Logical/mathematical** – the ability to reason, problem solve, think logically and use abstract concepts

As individuals we all have learning profiles that include many different types of 'intelligence'. Gardner's work is about balance. Many activities use several different types of intelligence. All need to be developed in all pupils. Pupils should not be 'pigeon-holed' to working in one area.

The following activities, which are all useful in RE, draw on different 'intelligences'. (An extended list can be found on page 21 of *REthinking book 2: Brain-based learning – lessons for RE*.) The 'intelligences' they may draw on are indicated in brackets.

Advice columns (1/6)
Analysing religious music/songs (2/7)
Calligrams (4)
Chat show (1/6)
Creating a database (1/7)
Creating displays (3/4)
Discussion (1/6)
Enacting phone calls (3)
Expressive dance (5/3)
Interviews (1/6)
Highlighting key words (7)
Life or feelings graphs (4/6)
Mime (5/3)
Musical journeys (2)
Newspaper reports (1)
Personal profiles (5/6)
Postcards/letters/diaries (1/6)
Prediction exercises (7)
Ranking exercises (7)
Sorting exercises (7)
Storyboard (4)
Story diagrams (4)
Writing lyrics (2/1)
Writing reflections/prayers (1/5)

6

2.4 Differentiation: learning styles – VAK

People learn in different ways or have preferred learning styles which they like to use, particularly for new or difficult material. However, all learners need to use all styles. Learners can be classified in different ways. VAK (visual, auditory and kinaesthetic) is only *one* form of classification and uses the senses.

- **Visual learners** like to see new information written or in picture form. They are good at visualising scenes.

- **Auditory learners** like to hear information and repeat it silently to themselves (internal talk). They enjoy talks, discussions and readings.

- **Kinaesthetic learners** like the physical and emotional sensations that come with learning. They learn best by doing and experiencing.

There are other classifications that identify four senses for learning (VATK and VARK) adding either the tactile as a separate mode from the kinaesthetic or splitting the visual into those who learn through pictures and images and those who relate to words. In this book we are using a simple three-way classification but teachers can explore the others by consulting the resources and websites listed on the resources page (inside back cover).

Awareness of different styles can help with differentiation by varying **input**. VAK is about balancing teaching styles over a unit, not necessarily doing everything in three ways. The suggestions that follow show different ways in which input can be varied. Some activities appear in two columns as they involve different styles. A sorting exercise can be visual if done on the board as a diagram, or kinaesthetic if objects or statements are written on card and manipulated. (An extended list can be found on page 19 of *REthinking book 2: Brain-based learning – lessons for RE.*)

Visual input	Auditory input	Kinaesthetic input
Banners/Posters	Case studies	Actions/signing
Cards	Debates	Brainstorming
Cartoons	Discussion in groups/pairs	Celebrations
Colour coding	Dramatic readings to music	Cooking/food
Diagrams/grids/graphs	Interviews/visitors	Dance/movement
Display	Metaphors and similes	Drama/mime/role-play
Illustrated books	Music/songs/hymns	Games
Images, art	Poetry	Interviews
Odd one out	Questions	Matching exercises
OHP/flip chart	Radio	Puppets
Puppets	Rap	Ranking/sorting exercises
Story bags	Sound effects to accompany readings	Response stories
Storyboards	Storytelling	Story bags
Symbols	Talks	Using or handling artefacts
Using objects/artefacts	Tapes/CDs	Using props
Videos		Visits
Visualisation		

7

REthinking

2.5 Differentiation: high level/low level tasks

In order to differentiate, it is important to know the difference between high-level and low-level tasks. A number of research projects have highlighted the low intellectual challenge that RE activities make of pupils. As long ago as the mid 1980's, Trevor Kerry[1] listed high-level and low-level tasks and showed that most tasks given to pupils in RE are low-level. Such tasks expose pupils to information without challenging them to do something with it. High-level tasks involve using information. Since Kerry's research, things have got better. There is, however, still room for improvement.

Some tasks, classified here as low-level, would be challenging for young/less able pupils. This does not mean that these pupils should not be given high-level tasks. The youngest pupil can be asked to do imaginative work or role-play the application of teaching to daily life. This table has been adapted from Trevor Kerry's original list. Think through your own RE lessons. How many high-level tasks do you include?

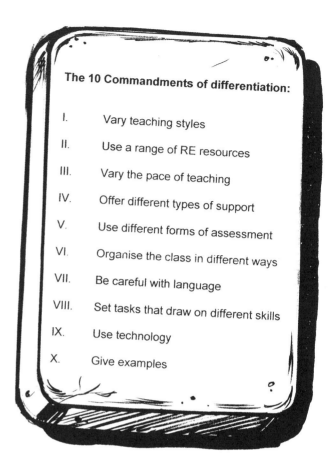

The 10 Commandments of differentiation:

I.   Vary teaching styles

II.   Use a range of RE resources

III.   Vary the pace of teaching

IV.   Offer different types of support

V.   Use different forms of assessment

VI.   Organise the class in different ways

VII.   Be careful with language

VIII.   Set tasks that draw on different skills

IX.   Use technology

X.   Give examples

Low-level tasks	High-level tasks
Silent reading/reading aloud	Synthesis tasks (e.g., bringing together sources/information)
Reinforcing/practising	Collecting evidence
Memorising	Imaginative activities
Revising/testing	Deducing
Cloze or comprehension work	Analysis tasks
Copying	Evaluation tasks
Looking up information	Application tasks
Drawing or colouring	Problem solving
Watching/listening	

[1]Kerry, Trevor, *Teaching Religious Education* (MacMillan 1984)

2.6 Seven different ways to differentiate in RE

When considering differentiation, it can be classified in various ways, for example:

- **Input (I)** – what the RE teacher or resources put in
- **Outcome (O)** – the end result
- **Process (P)** – the means used to achieve the outcome

Note. The term 'outcome' is used in education with slightly different meanings. It is sometimes used to mean the end result in terms of a product, which might be writing, a poster or a poem. It also means end result in terms of understanding and skills. An example of this latter meaning is a learning outcome, e.g.,"By the end of this RE unit pupils should be able to ..." Teachers should bear this in mind when reading this section.

Content – the material (I)

Content in RE is often largely determined by Agreed Syllabuses, government guidelines (Scotland and Northern Ireland) and school schemes of work. However, within that there is some leeway. For example, if 'parables' is the broad heading there is still some choice, as some parables are more difficult than others.

Assessment/Response – how teachers assess or respond (O)

Teacher response should reflect pupil achievement. This can be in a variety of forms, from oral responses to written reports. It can include video, audio tapes and review sheets. Use review sheets with pictures. For younger and less able pupils, reduce the amount of writing on review sheets and use ticks instead. Make RE objectives clear and, if necessary, set individual or group targets.

Resources – what pupils use (I/P)

RE books/worksheets should be well designed and structured, be at the appropriate level and easy to use. Resources should have appropriate illustrations that engage pupils. This is important in RE as pupils often have strong stereotypes. Material can be presented in a variety of forms, e.g., videos, CD-ROMs, drama, and artefacts.

Task – what pupils do (P)

Tasks should be set at different levels and vary in complexity, media, skills required and styles. National RE guidelines should be used for this. Tasks should match abilities, from pupils with learning difficulties to gifted and talented pupils. Allowing choice in tasks gives room for differentiation.

Outcome – the end result (O)

The *form* of the outcome (product) as well as the quality and quantity can vary. Pupils can be offered different ways to present the results of a task. The amount and level of work pupils produce can also be varied. This latter can be unsatisfactory if over-used. It means some pupils never get to the end of a piece of work.

Pace (P)

The speed at which pupils are taught or expected to work can be varied.

Support – how much help pupils have (I/P)

This help may be in the form of adults, such as the teacher, specialist supporter (LSA, mentor), or parents. It could also be support by collaborative work with fellow pupils or by computer or other technology. Word banks and writing frames are also a form of support.

Something to think about

You can choose just **one** of these at a time! If you wish, you can add the word **CARTOPS** to your lesson plans and tick which type of differentiation you are using. (Explain it somewhere in your folder.)

2.7 Class organisation and differentiation

The way a class is organised and how the tasks are assigned is part of differentiation. The following draws on Chris Dickinson's categories detailed in his book *A Practical Handbook of Classroom Strategies – Differentiation* (see resources page for more information).

Individual tasks

- All pupils work at their own level *each* on different assignments within a given subject. Example: Pupils do individual work on Sikhism.

One task

- One task is set by the teacher but the *amount* (quantity) pupils complete varies. Example: Writing a report on visiting a Mosque.
- All do the same task but with varying *levels* of achievement (the quality and depth varies). Material may be aimed at the 'average' pupil. Example: All pupils are asked to explain the five precepts of Buddhism.

Tasks set at different levels/with different product outcomes

The teacher sets a standard task with variations for the most and least able (basic, standard and extension). Example: Pupils are asked to describe, in writing, the way Jesus is portrayed in a video and evaluate the portrayal. A <u>basic</u> task would allow the task to be done using a Dictaphone and a simple evaluation question. An <u>extension</u> task might ask pupils to compare one film with another.

- A core set of activities is given for all to do with number of options (not just extension and basic). Example: The core activity might be classifying the Ten Commandments in Judaism into those that directly relate to God and those that relate to other people. The options could be: How they are celebrated in worship in Judaism, how they are practised in daily life, the values they express, how they relate to the law of the land.

- The teacher sets a series of tasks finely graded so that only the most able will reach the top level. For example,
  - ◆ Read the story of the good Samaritan
  - ◆ Underline key words
  - ◆ Write/say why they are important
  - ◆ Write a version of the story for younger pupils using simpler words in place of the key words.
  - ◆ Analyse why this story is important to Christians today

Group work

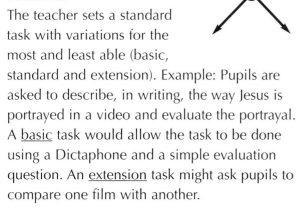

- Students work in mixed ability groups, supporting each other, e.g., working together on a booklet to explain Divali.
- Single ability groups can be given work of appropriate difficulty. Example: Pupils research the work of a local faith community in the area.
- Interest groups can be formed for a particular task. The teacher supplies a variety of tasks and the pupils choose and form groups. Example: A series of tasks related to the Bible: different genre, how it was passed on, how it is used by Christians, original languages, translations, etc.

2.8 Differentiation and RE worksheets

RE worksheets are often criticised because they make few demands and lack differentiation. The following may help in designing challenging worksheets:

- Where possible, separate task and content/information so that you have more space to differentiate. Put the information/story on one sheet and the tasks on another. This also means that the same RE story/information can be used many times with different task sheets.

- If you do have questions/tasks and information on the same sheet, put the questions/task before the information so that pupils read with a purpose in mind.

- Separating the tasks and information allows for differentiation by resource. Resources can be indicated on the worksheet and pupils directed to particular resources depending on ability.

- Add prompts, word bank and things to think about if there is room.

- Put the outcome on the worksheet so that pupils know what they need to achieve. ("By the end of this unit/session you should have produced . . .") Check what you are expecting them to do against your scheme of work and your RE criteria (levels, etc.).

- Increase graphics on worksheets for younger pupils and pupils with learning difficulties.

- Include some assessment criteria on the sheet so that pupils know what the teacher will be looking for. Use RE criteria (levels, etc.) to inform this; your assessment is then integral to your teaching and easy to check/evaluate afterwards.

- Reduce words and increase 'white space' on worksheets to allow teachers to customise them to specific individuals/groups. Worksheets can either be supplied and adapted electronically or provided on paper and adapted by hand, writing comments and instructions in the white space.

- White space can also be used by teachers to record that spoken tasks have been completed if pupils have difficulty writing. It can also be used for assessment comments, transferring comments from previous work, pupil comments or for target setting (see page 20).

- List differentiated tasks on the worksheet allowing for choice where possible.

Note. On the example worksheet that follows on page 12, teacher handwriting is indicated by italics.

> **Handy hint**: If appropriate for your age group, leave a 'white space' big enough for a post-it note. Your comments can be added to the post-it note, meaning the sheet can be reused many times. You can jot assessment notes on them as you move round checking work and then peel them off and add to your folder or transfer the notes to your folder. Remember to put the name of the group on the post-it note.

11

REthinking

Sample worksheet: Easter

This unit is about Easter. I want you to read the Easter story and complete the tasks below.

By the end of this unit you should be able to do a short group presentation on Easter. Include what is important about the Easter story for Christians and some of the symbols used by them.

I will be looking for evidence that shows you understand the story and the meaning of important words and symbols.

Tasks
1. Read the story of Easter.
2. Tick or list six important words.
3. Say or write why they are important.
4. Find out about the meaning of some of the symbols of Easter.
5. Include your important words and symbols in a group presentation of the story.

You could present your work as:
A. A poster with notes that you show and explain
B. A written report that you read
C. A talk with some notes and illustrations

Red group

*Use the **books** rather than the sheets.*

***Write** why the words are important.*

Resources

Symbols sheet
The Easter story sheet
Children's Bibles
Signs and symbols book
Festival book

Important words

| cross | crucifixion | resurrection | Jesus | disciple | death |

| life | sorrow | joy |

2.9 Quick reference for planning differentiated learning

The next few pages summarise much of the information so far. Photocopy them and use them as a quick reference when planning. Once you have selected your RE material, think about the children you teach, and then look under the different headings and select a way of differentiating.

2.10 Differentiation for younger or less able pupils

The suggestions that follow are only guidelines. To adapt material for younger or less able pupils, the following criteria *may* be used:

Easier – Resource/Content/Task/Outcome
Choose an easier subject/task/resource/outcome, e.g., choose a story from a sacred text in easy language or select a simpler religious idea. Staff may wish to choose material meant for younger pupils for some less able pupils, as long as the material itself is 'age appropriate'. Tasks and Outcomes can be less demanding in the following areas: Creative skills, cognitive skills, motor skills, emotional skills (e.g., empathy). However, these areas should not be neglected. It is only a matter of degree.

Less – Resource/Content/Task/Outcome/Pace
The teacher can give less information about a religion. Pupils are given less to do in order to complete the task or to present in the outcome. Pupils may also work in groups or in pairs so that they each do part of a task rather than are responsible for completing all of it.

Slower – Pace
Work is delivered and completed at a slower rate.

Less abstract/more concrete – Content/Resources
With younger or less able pupils it is particularly important that concepts should be linked to their experience, to practical examples or embedded in stories that they can understand. Alternatively, first hand experiences can be created in the classroom or visits can be arranged. Reflections should be simple and with a concrete focus – a candle, a rock.

Simpler language level – Resources
Difficult words can be explained or replaced but pupils should build up a specialist religious vocabulary. Specialist words should be heard, displayed, highlighted in texts and used in context. Word lists or word banks can be supplied on worksheets or as part of an RE display, e.g., Allah, Hajj, Ka'aba, Qur'an. The questions teachers ask should be appropriate for the age level. Simplify and repeat as necessary.

Different forms – Resources/Tasks/Outcome
Resources should appeal to the senses. Use religious artefacts, video, role-play, etc. Use alternatives to writing sometimes, e.g., drama, diagrams, art and visitors from the local religious community. Work can be recorded on a Dictaphone if pupils have problems writing, and word processing packages can be used to add pictures/symbols to text to act as visual clues.

REthinking

Restrict the sources – Sources
Reduce the number of sources the pupils are expected to use at the same time, e.g., limit to a book or a worksheet or a video with a worksheet.

More support – Support
The teacher, other adults and pupils (pairs, groups) can give additional support, or ICT can be used. Word lists and definitions are also a support. Use computers as they are a 'patient' technology – there is more than one chance to get it right. Use computer design packages to get over problems with drawing/writing and use keyboard overlays and touch screens.

Less individual work – Task/Outcome
Class activities allow the individual to contribute without being solely responsible for completing a task. Group activities (mixed ability groups) and paired activities (mixed ability pairs) allow for peer support. Pupils can offer part of a presentation or piece of work.

More structured – Task
The younger or less able the pupil, the more structured tasks need to be. Writing frames can

be used in RE and templates for note taking. (The fifth book in the *REthinking* series: *Planning challenging RE lessons* gives examples of these.)

Avoid multiple skills – Task
Younger or less able pupils need tasks with only one or two skills (listen, draw).

More descriptive/less evaluative – Task
Some 'Why do you think?' questions can be used at all levels. Basic evaluation tasks and simple ways of exploring meaning and significance of beliefs can be included. Teachers can set tasks that require pupils to respond to the beliefs, feelings and experiences of others without analysing that response too deeply. Simple identification, describing, recounting or listing tasks can be used but pupils should not be limited to these. They can present basic outlines and key features of a religion rather than detailed material.

Simple links – Task
Use simple tasks that involve pupils in making some links within a religion and between religions, e.g., between belief and its expression in behaviour and religious celebrations.

Well focused – Task
Tasks or questions that are *too* open-ended can leave some pupils floundering. Pupils need to know what is required of them. That does not mean limiting younger or less able pupils to closed questions.

Some things to remember

Teachers will need to:

- Consolidate and reinforce material
- Adapt material appropriately
- Make full use of the senses in the way information and experience is given and in the way tasks are designed
- Use aids where ever possible, e.g., large print books
- Pupils who have problems reading and writing may have talent in RE. Differentiation should enable them to express those abilities.

2.11 Differentiation for older or more able pupils

Harder – Content/Resources/Tasks/Outcome

Choose a harder and more challenging subject/resource/task/outcome. For example, look at difficult issues such as different ideas about the afterlife. Set tasks that encourage pupils to create complex questions raised by the material. Tasks can be demanding in the following skills: cognitive, creative, emotional, and motor. Gifted pupils should be able to work with primary source material.

More abstract/less concrete – Content/Task

Give more conceptual work on difficult ideas, e.g., reincarnation, sacrifice. Set work that explores the meaning and significance of religious language and symbolism. Create tasks that involve identifying influences and more abstract aspects of RE. Tasks should be less descriptive and more analytic and evaluative, focusing on fundamental questions that lie beneath religious stories and practices. Encourage pupils to transfer ideas from one context to another. Create a range of reflections, *not always* with a tangible focus. More abstract reflections can be used.

Faster – Pace

Increase the pace at which you teach and at which the pupils work on a task.

Multiple points of view – Resource/Task

Explore various people's stances, e.g., creating a diagram of the parable of the prodigal son, showing the perspectives of the father, the younger and the older brother. Set tasks that require understanding issues from the point of view of the religion studied, e.g., how Jesus is viewed by Jews.

Less/different support – Support

Use less or different types of adult support. This might include using visitors from a faith community as a source of support for extension work for a high ability group. Pupils can create their own word lists and definitions. (Some support can be supplied through appropriate dictionaries, reference books and the Internet.)

More individual work or challenging group work – Support

Individual pupils can be responsible for a whole piece of work or do more work in high ability pairs/groups that challenge and stimulate. They can work with older pupils.

Less structure – Tasks

RE questions and tasks can be more open-ended. Pupils can be left with some latitude to work out *how* to complete the task although what is expected of them still needs to be made clear. Gifted pupils may be able to define their own tasks.

More/deeper – Tasks/Outcome

Give pupils more information and more to do in order to complete the task and expect more in the outcome and in greater depth. However, depth rather than just more work at the same level is to be preferred. Pupils should be making deeper connections between values, beliefs and behaviour and looking in depth at meaning and significance.

Multiple skills – Tasks

Older pupils can do complex tasks that involve multiple skills, e.g., analyse the design on a banner from a local church. Pupils can write what ideas and feelings it expresses and design their own banner to express those ideas.

Less descriptive/more evaluative and interpretative – Tasks

Encourage pupils to form opinions and evaluate material, being able to justify their thinking and providing evidence and criteria for making judgements. E.g., evaluating the decisions characters make in religious stories (Moses, Buddha).

Higher language level – Resource/Task

Include words that pupils will have to look up and define. Include more specialist vocabulary, e.g., Dharma, Bodhi, bodhisattava, samsara, mandala. Help able pupils to develop the specialist language to help them think through difficult religious and moral issues.

Different forms – Resource/Task

Use difficult forms drawing on different types of learning and intelligence, e.g., writing poetry, composing music, problem solving and discussing difficult religious/ethical issues. Able pupils should present material to the whole class/group using appropriate technology and the appropriate specialist vocabulary. They should organise and present results in a variety of ways and demonstrate ability by using some of he following skills:

- Communicating two sides of an argument
- Taking account of the needs of a particular audience
- Using different styles: reports, etc.
- Expressing different view points
- Using persuasive arguments
- Using summaries and overviews
- Offering answers to difficult questions by drawing on their own or other's experience

Multiple sources – Resources

Use different sources together, e.g., a religious text with a poem and a painting, and ask pupils to assess the way in which the artist, writer and poet have interpreted the same subject. Use sources where opinions differ. Set pupils tasks where they have to synthesise several sources.

More links – Tasks

Link RE to other subjects (History, geography, science) and connect RE to the wider world (current affairs). Explore links between a range of texts and artefacts. Encourage pupils to make more complex links between faith, life style and worship.

Wider ranging – Tasks

This can be in the form of overviews, comparisons and summaries, e.g., comparisons and contrasts of initiation ceremonies in several religions.

Older or more able pupils

17

Some things to remember

- A pupil might be gifted in RE but not in other subjects so it is still important to use a variety of forms. Remember that a pupil may be gifted in any of the seven (or more) areas of 'intelligence' (see page 6 for more details).

- Gifted pupils need a variety of challenging, questioning strategies ("What if . . .?") and the use of higher order thinking skills (predict, analyse, etc.).

- They can explore how religious ideas can be applied in a range of different contexts.

- They need differentiation by dialogue – using more complex language.

- Gifted pupils should not only be stretched intellectually. The whole person should be challenged.

- Use demanding approaches such as 'Thinking Skills'.

3.1 Assessment – the basics

Not everything in RE has to be assessed. Not everything that has been assessed has to be formally recorded and reported. How much assessment and recording is used is up to each school. With an Agreed Syllabus or National Guidelines and a scheme of work in place, teachers can also reduce the amount they write. They do not have to write what has been taught – they can refer to the scheme of work. Teachers only have to write what has been achieved.

Attainment Targets and levels are crucial for assessment as they provide teachers with criteria to measure pupil work against.

For assessment to work, it must be an integral part of learning and teaching, not an 'add on'. It should be non-threatening, relevant, clearly presented and worth doing. There must be shared goals and it should reflect classroom practice, pupil experience and build on what has been learned. An assessment task should test RE and allow pupils to demonstrate their knowledge and understanding. To this end, tasks should be varied so that not only reading and writing are tested.

Assessment is about making evaluations determined by different types of evidence which then becomes the basis for decisions about pupil needs and future work. Assessment happens all the time, not just at the end of a unit of work and it can be formal or informal.

When recording the results of assessment, five factors need to be remembered:

1. Keep it simple – limit the assessment objectives at the planning stage
2. Keep it appropriate – for the pupils and the context
3. Keep it accessible – can others understand it?
4. Keep it meaningful – is it worth doing?
5. Include all the relevant information

More art than science

As the different learning objectives vary, so does assessment, There are some precise objectives in RE that cover knowledge and understanding that can be tested in a reasonably precise way (e.g., do they know the five pillars of Islam?). The more personal side of religion (Learning from religion/Personal Search/Awareness, Exploration and Response) have objectives that involve pupil awareness and sensitivity that cannot be assessed in the same way.

Information for assessment

Information for assessment comes from three areas; all can be used in RE:
- General observation
- Specific observation for a purpose
- Set tasks where pupils demonstrate learning

The Process

There are four stages involved in assessing pupils:
- Deciding on the RE knowledge/skills to be assessed, e.g., Islam
- Creating the task that will assess the RE knowledge, e.g., role-play, review sheet, poster
- Working out a way to present the task. Make sure it is testing RE and not just reading skills (although oral and written instructions may be appropriate for some groups)
- How evidence is going to be collected, e.g., video, writing, tapes, photos

The Tasks

Assessment tasks should be worthwhile and allow pupils to show what they can do. Make sure they challenge thinking rather than just ask pupils to repeat facts. Don't just 'teach to the test'.

RE**th**inking

Target setting

After a piece of work has been assessed teachers can discuss with pupils how to improve their work. Assessment informs target setting and setting targets in turn helps with assessment. The process is mutual. Targets must be realistic and achievable and they should be linked to specific skills in RE.

Individual/group

Most formal assessment is individual but some RE can be assessed as a group, e.g., drama. This can be difficult, however, as some individuals may contribute a lot, others may do very little. Many teachers comment on the group project then make notes about individual contributions: script, planning, etc.

Sarah, to gain a higher level, you need to present other people's viewpoints, not just your own.

Owen, you need to apply what you have learned by giving examples of how this religious teaching might apply in practice.

3.2 Varying the assessment task

Assessment must take account of differentiation. We differentiate in the way that we teach by using a variety of methods such as drama, art and poetry. Assessment tasks should be differentiated as well. Assessment should reflect not only what the pupils have learned, but the way in which they have learned it. Assessment can vary in style but when choosing bear in mind the time factor. Videos and audio tapes can be time consuming to evaluate.

RE is a rich and complex subject. There is a temptation, however, to assess only the factual side of the subject. Much more of RE can be assessed providing the appropriate type of task is used. Pupils can demonstrate their understanding through:

Music

Pupils can create lyrics and compositions with accompanying explanations, e.g., putting new RE words to a well-known song tune. Pupils can create music to express their understanding and response.

Booklets

Booklets can combine writing and pictures. This can be in the form of a reflective diary where pupils have a range of questions and tasks, and room to make their own comments in a small booklet. Such booklets can cover knowledge and understanding, and feelings and values. **Note**. Pupils should only be asked to include those feelings and responses they are happy to disclose.

Photographs/pictures/art

Give pupils a photograph, picture, symbol or image related to the subject that has been studied, e.g., Communion. Ask pupils to write questions about the faith and thoughts of the people in the photograph/picture. The questions should reflect their understanding of the situation shown in the picture.

Matching exercises

Matching exercises can be used for a quick assessment. Can pupils match statements or captions to pictures?

Artefacts

Use a tray of artefacts and ask pupils to tell you (or write) what they know about each one or classify them in some way. Alternatively, for some types of assessment you can ask them to add what they would like to know.

Statements

Give pupils a range of statements and ask who is most likely to say them and why (Muslim, Christian, etc.) Reasons should be given for choices.

Posters

Ask pupils to create a poster using text and images to convey their understanding of a topic, e.g., the key beliefs of Buddhism.

21

Book 6: Planning for effective learning in RE

Videos

Pupils can create a video presentation on a subject, e.g., marriage ceremonies in different religions.

Games

Various games, including simple board games, can be devised to test pupil knowledge and understanding of RE. If pupils devise their own questions this could also cover the affective side of RE.

Ranking ranking diamond

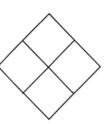

Use a ranking arrow or diamond to assess a pupil's understanding of an issue. Ask them to rank things according to the values of a particular faith community. This might also be linked to their own reflections and values.

Brainstorm

At the end of a unit of work, give pupils questions as a stimulus for brainstorming that reflects knowledge and understanding of religious beliefs and the more affective side of teaching. For example: Why do Christians celebrate Easter? What sacrifices do we make? The brainstorm can be done on individual sheets of paper or as groups with different pupils using different coloured pencils to record their suggestions.

Drama

Use role-play, sketches, enactments, improvisation, mock telephone calls, mime and dance for assessment.

Sequencing

Give pupils a series of pictures, speeches or thoughts and ask them to sequence them in order to establish that they have understood a story or ritual, e.g., Passover.

Design

Design activities should be chosen that allow pupils to express their learning and their response to it, e.g., posters, logos, T-shirts, video covers and book jackets.

Questions

Ask pupils to write/say the answers or they can design both the questions and the answers. Give older pupils a set of answers and ask them to create the questions.

Writing

Writing can cover answering questions, reflective diaries, poems, reports, leaflets, postcards, articles, letters, dictionary entries, essays, keywords and stories.

Oral response

Oral responses can be made through discussion and conversation with the teachers and their peers, through oral presentations and recorded responses (preparing a tape).

Varying the assessment task

22

Mind or concept maps

Mind or concept 'maps' can be used in a variety of ways: as a starter, half way through a topic so that you can see where the gaps are in pupils understanding and for assessment at the end. You can use them at both the start and the end of a topic so that you get a clear idea of what pupils have learned. To make a concept map:

1. Write the concept or subject in the centre: Judaism

2. Around it, write the main headings or keywords as thick 'branches'. (These are normally fairly general or abstract in character. Don't have too many, e.g., festivals, worship, beliefs, lifestyle

3. Draw thinner 'twigs' (sub branches) for things contained under the main headings. Use single words or short phrases where possible. (Items on the 'twigs' tend to be more concrete and specific.)

4. Add images, pictures, diagrams, symbols, etc.

Pupils can be asked to fill in an incomplete mind map as an assessment task.

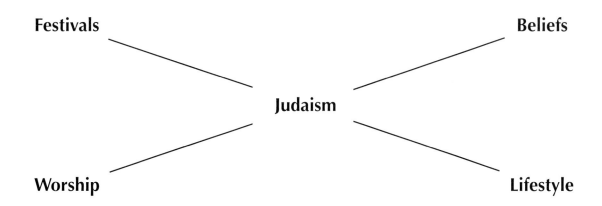

3.3 Different forms of assessment

Assessment for different purposes

Assessment can be for different purposes. Some are listed below. It is important to use the right assessment tool for the purpose you have in mind. This book only deals with the types of assessment teachers use most often in RE.

- Base line assessment – what they already know, e.g., about Buddhism
- IQ tests – what a child might achieve
- Diagnostic assessment – locating problems a pupil may have
- Formative assessment – what they are learning and how teaching may need to change, e.g., how much they have understood about the festival of Divali
- Norm referenced assessment – how they are performing in relation to their peers
- Criterion referenced assessment – how they are performing in regard to set criterion (levels, grading systems)
- Summative assessment – something of what a child has learned, e.g., about Sikhism

Assessment by omission

Teachers don't have to write comments for every single pupil. The end of unit expectations on the QCA schemes of work provide descriptions of attainment for three broad groups. Teachers can note where a pupil's achievement differs from the rest of the class. Alternatively, just write on your short-term plan those pupils who found a task too difficult or too easy.

Peer assessment/ Response partners

Pupils can respond to each other's work but they will need guidance on what to say and a firm structure to work with. They need

criteria and they need to know what success looks like or work will be difficult to evaluate. It is helpful to have a list of useful phrases for pupils to choose from. Pupils need to point out what is good and how work can be improved. Ground rules need to be established. However, peer group assessment can also be fun and can get pupils involved.

Observation

This has always been part of teacher assessment. By observation, teachers can assess what a child can do in all sorts of situations that are not easy to reproduce in a formal test. Formal observation, however, needs a clear purpose and all observation requires a restricted focus (know what you are looking for).

Oral evaluation

The teacher engages in discussion with pupils after telling a story or using an RE stimulus. RE criteria should be borne in mind so that teachers have something to assess pupils against. Oral assessment can also take the form of interviews and question and answer sessions.

Formal tests

These can be in various formats: multiple choice, complete the sentences, answer the questions, essays or structured activities. (However, bear in mind expectations.)

RE portfolio

This is an ongoing collection showing samples of work for each pupil; work that reflects significant achievement, progress, a range of activities, and fulfilment of attainment targets. It should be updated annually but does not need to include a huge number of samples. It can include posters, photographs and tapes as well as writing.

Review sheets

Several examples of these are included both below and on pages 27-30. They can be arranged in a number of ways. They can be illustrated and can include drawn answers.

Infant review sheet

In one 'person' write the good things that people did in the story of the good Samaritan.

In the other 'person' write the bad things that people did in the story of the good Samaritan.

Underneath write the good things you could do.

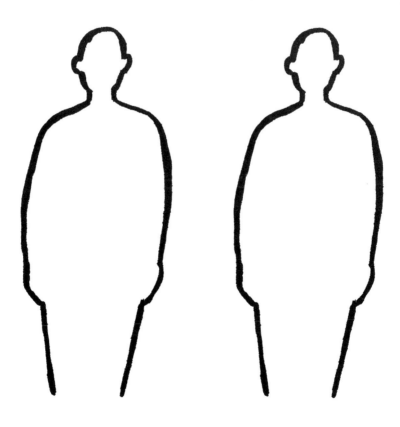

Self correction/self marking

This is useful for assessing factual information. The pupils are given an answer sheet to use. This cannot be used on ambiguous material.

Marking and teacher comments

Marking and teacher comments are a form of continuous (formative) assessment. Marking gives pupils quick feedback on progress and can pick up problems early. Marking should reflect both attainment and effort. The policy on marking can be put on a poster so that pupils know what grades mean and what will be marked and what may not be corrected or commented on. Some secondary teachers have a standard list of comments displayed with grades by them.

Example:
1. Excellent
2. Very good
3. Good

Grading structures can be added to self-assessment sheets for older pupils so that pupils have their own assessment and the teacher's assessment.

Pupils care about teacher comments. Able pupils tend to benefit more from what the teacher says than marks or grades. They want comments that are truthful and challenging. They want constructive criticism.

Record cards

Record cards are kept for many subjects. They can be kept for RE but not all pieces of work need be recorded.

Formative, summative and self-assessment

These are dealt with separately – see pages 27-30.

RE Profiles

The profile can be one sheet of A4 folded to make a 'diary' (8 A6 sides) with assessment tasks that are filled in as the unit progresses. It can contain some of the following:

• Formative assessment tasks
• A final summative task
• Self assessment
• Teacher assessment
• Some reflective tasks

The tasks should cover both the affective and cognitive aspect of RE. The diary can be printed, cut and folded so that there is a minimum of writing.

Note: Profiles can cover different things. This is only one form.

3.4 Formative assessment

This is a continuous process integral to all learning and teaching. It includes marking, comments on work, self-evaluation, oral responses and target setting. It is often diagnostic and allows remedy – pointing out what is good and how it could be improved. It helps the teacher plan for future learning. The difference between summative and formative assessment is largely in intention. Formative assessment is intended to improve learning; summative assessment is meant to inform about student progress. In practice the boundaries are blurred. A wide variety of styles can be used for formative assessment. Some people use review sheets. A sample is included.

Note: Below, selected sections of assessment sheets are shown and they are reduced in size for reasons of space.

Islam

Three things I know about Islam:

1.   . . . .

2.   . . . .

3.   . . . .

I think prayer is important to Muslims because . . . .

One comment I want to make about prayer . . . .

A book I find useful is . . . .

I enjoy learning about . . . .

I am finding . . . . **difficult.**

One thing I have learned so far that helps me to understand others . . . .

REthinking

3.5 Summative assessment

Summative assessment summarises and reports on what has been learned. One way of doing it is to use a situation.

"Sarah has not been able to go to school, as she has been ill. She wants to know what we have been studying. I have given you a sheet with some headings. I want you to tell Sarah what she has missed using these headings as a guide."

"We are doing an assembly on Sikhism. What do we need to include in order to help people understand the Sikh faith and what it means to Sikhs?"

Imaginary situations can also be used with younger pupils. Try using a soft toy or puppet or an imaginary pupil as a fun way of doing assessment.

"Zak the Zebra wants to know what you have learned about Christmas."

A wide variety of styles can be used for summative assessment. Some people use review sheets, for example:

Sikhism

Symbols

This is the symbol of . . . .

It means . . . .

This is a . . . .

It is special for Sikhs because . . . .

This is a . . . .

It represents . . . .

The sacred text of the Sikhs is called . . . .

It is important to Sikhs because . . . .

I show my commitment by . . . .

3.6 Self assessment

Pupils can assess their own learning, but it is sometimes useful to give them a sheet with headings or a set of questions. Alternatively a review sheet can be created using words or pictures or a mixture of both. Self assessment sheets need to be visual for younger pupils – ticks can then be placed in appropriate columns. Starter phrases and word boxes can also be supplied to help young pupils with written evaluations.

Young pupils may find self assessment difficult to begin with as they have little experience of evaluation. Teenagers may also find it difficult and either understate or overstate their achievement, depending on personality.

A wide variety of styles can be used for self assessment. Some people use review sheets, for example:

Starter phrases

I made/did . . .

I liked/disliked . . .

I used . . .

I remember . . .

I already know . . .

I would like to find out more about . . .

. . . surprised me

. . . was interesting

I would like to ask . . .

I was pleased with . . .

I worked with . . .

It took me . . .

Junior self assessment sheet

Easter

I liked . . . . best.

I liked . . . . least.

I found . . . . difficult because . . . .

X made me think . . . .

X made me feel . . . .

I think my best piece of work was . . . .

I would like to find out more about . . . .

I can improve by . . . .

I think Easter is important to Christians because . . . .

Infant self assessment

Pupils add faces according to how well they think they have done. Faces can be drawn or stuck on.

Activity: Lost Son (Luke 15) Year 1	Well	Could be better	Not very well
Creative (writing)	🙂		
Role-play	🙂		
Picture based on a painting		😐	

REthinking

3.7 Issues in assessment

What's the point?

Why bother assessing? There are four reasons and all of them apply to RE in some form but in differing degrees.

1. Accountability – in order to report to the parents and society at large
2. Selection – some tests select for further or different types of education
3. Motivation – pupils need to see their progress
4. Information – to give knowledge about the learning and teaching that has been occurring

In RE motivation and information are particularly important as they are the ones that, properly handled, can enhance RE and improve teaching and learning.

What does assessment tell us in RE?

Assessment only tells us some things about a pupil's ability and in RE it only tells us about their understanding of part of the subject. Assessment can tell us something of what they already know, might achieve, are learning, have learned or how they are performing in relation to their peers or a set of criterion.

What *can* be tested in RE?

Factual knowledge can be tested, but RE is more than that. There are also beliefs, skills, attitudes and values. We can note the presence or absence of certain attitudes, particularly attitudes towards learning in RE but not on a progressive scale. It would also be invasive to assess beliefs and values although we can assess the process and skills used to arrive at those beliefs and values.

Some examples of comments on skills and attitudes:

- Anna listens well and contributes well to discussions
- Callum tries to understand other people's beliefs
- Ellen can link religious belief and her own experience
- Steven can express his own beliefs well

What *can't* be tested in RE?

RE has an 'affective' element (Learning from religion/Personal Search/Awareness, Exploration and Response) some of which may be not only difficult to assess but inappropriate to assess. RE is not alone in that – many subjects have areas that are difficult to test.

Lat Blaylock[2] suggests that in RE you cannot test:

- The importance of personal belief and commitment to high ideals
- Personal purpose, vision and determination to follow good ends
- Whether pupils apply what they have learned to their own lives
- How far respectful attitudes are internalised
- If they are increasingly at ease with ambiguity and complexity
- How much they empathise with those who are different/vulnerable
- Their response to temptation and challenges to faith
- How far they draw on their personal resources when facing suffering
- Their moral and spiritual development

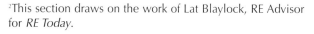

Although these may not be assessed formally, when indication of any of the above does occur, they can be acknowledged and affirmed. This does not mean that teachers should stick to testing the facts and ignore the broader aspects of RE. Providing an appropriately broad range of tasks are used, much (but not all) of the subject can be assessed.

[2]This section draws on the work of Lat Blaylock, RE Advisor for *RE Today*.

3.8 Some concluding thoughts

All assessment is flawed in the sense that it depends on the judgements and observations of human beings and the validity of tests can always be questioned – they only measure the measurable. There are other drawbacks:

- Pupils often know far more than they are able to articulate
- Assessment demotivates *some* pupils. Some pupils relax if they do well and stop trying
- Assessment may discourage others if they have done badly
- Assessment can be a self fulfilling prophecy; pupils can live up to the results and feel labelled

No assessment exercise is perfect, but the perfect should not get in the way of the possible. The human element is also a strength, people can

spot insights presented in unorthodox ways. There are other positive aspects to assessment:

- Knowing they will be assessed motivates some pupils
- Pupils like feedback
- Regular continuous assessment can improve learning
- Assessment can give us valuable information that improves teaching, keeps parents informed and give pupils a sense of progress.

In conclusion, assessment is a valuable tool that should serve, not drive RE teaching and it should be adapted to suit the nature of the subject. RE is different to Maths or English and the assessment should match the content. An appropriate set of assessment activities is more important than pin-point accuracy.